Michael Blystone

Pirates Code to Life and Leadership

The Pirates Code to Life and Leadership

Prologue

The pirate's code is not just a set of rules for seafarers of yesteryear, it is a timeless philosophy that still holds value in our modern world. At its core, the pirate's code emphasizes freedom, loyalty, bravery, and cunning - values that are as relevant today as they were centuries ago. Living by the pirate's code means embracing an adventurous spirit, living with purpose, and being true to oneself and one's crew. These principles can serve as a model for anyone looking to live a life filled with excitement and meaning. By embracing the values of the pirate's code, we can learn to live our lives to the fullest, take risks, and chase our dreams with determination. So, whether you're setting sail on the open seas or navigating life's challenges on dry land, remember the lessons of the pirate's code and chart a course towards a life full of adventure and purpose.

"Dead men tell no tales, but if ye be brave enough to listen, the secrets of the sea can be yours."

- Edward Teach, better known as Blackbeard.

Chapter 1: What Is the Pirates Code?

The pirates code is a set of guidelines and principles that govern the behavior of pirates and serve as a blueprint for living a life of adventure and leadership. It is not a set of strict laws, but rather a set of principles that pirates abide by in order to survive and thrive in the harsh and unpredictable world of piracy.

The code is based on the idea that in order for a pirate crew to succeed, all members must work together and trust each other. This is achieved through mutual respect, fairness, and a willingness to take risks and make sacrifices for the greater good of the crew. One of the most famous examples of this principle in action is the pirate crew of Edward Teach, also known as Blackbeard. Blackbeard was known for his fair and just leadership, and his crew was one of the most loyal and successful in pirate history.

The code also emphasizes the importance of personal freedom and individuality. Pirates are not bound by the rules and conventions of society, and are free to pursue their own goals and ambitions. This sense of freedom is central to the pirate lifestyle, and is reflected in the code's emphasis on independence, self-reliance, and self-expression. Famous pirate Anne Bonny is a perfect example of this principle in action, as she was one of the few female pirates and lived her life on her own terms, defying societal expectations of women at the time.

In addition to these core principles, the pirates code also includes specific rules and guidelines for the day-to-day operations of a pirate crew. These include guidelines for the distribution of loot, the handling of prisoners, and the resolution of disputes among crew members. For example, the pirate Bartholomew Roberts, also known as Black Bart, was known for his strict adherence to these rules and for his fair distribution of loot among his crew.

Overall, the pirates code is a set of principles and guidelines that have been passed down through generations of pirates, and continue to shape the lives and leadership styles of many today. It is a testament to the spirit of adventure and the desire for freedom that has always been at the heart of the pirate lifestyle. Famous pirates such as Blackbeard, Anne Bonny, and Black Bart are just a few examples of how these principles have been put into action throughout history and continue to inspire modern-day leaders and individuals alike.

"Every decision you make affects everyone around you, so you must live with the consequences of your actions. Take what ye want, but remember: everything comes at a price."
- *Anne Bonny*

Chapter 2: Principles of the Pirates Code

The pirates code is a set of principles that govern the behavior of pirates and serve as a blueprint for living a life of adventure and leadership. These principles are based on the idea that in order for a pirate crew to succeed, all members must work together and trust each other. In this chapter, we will examine some of the key principles of the pirates code and how they apply to leadership and daily life.

1. Fairness and mutual respect:

One of the most important principles of the pirates code is fairness and mutual respect. This means that all crew members are treated equally and with respect, regardless of their rank or status. This principle is essential for building trust and loyalty among the crew. Famous pirate Edward Teach, also known as Blackbeard, was known for his fair and just leadership, and his crew was one of the most loyal and successful in pirate history.

2. Self-reliance and independence:

Pirates are not bound by the rules and conventions of society, and are free to pursue their own goals and ambitions. This sense of freedom is reflected in the code's emphasis on self-reliance and independence. Famous pirate Anne Bonny is a perfect example of this principle in action, as she was one of the few female pirates and lived her life on her own terms, defying societal expectations of women.

3.   Risk-taking and sacrifice:

Pirates must be willing to take risks and make sacrifices in order to achieve their goals. This principle is reflected in the code's emphasis on courage and daring. Famous pirate William Kidd, also known as Captain Kidd, is a prime example of this principle in action, as he was known for his bold and daring raids and his willingness to take risks for the benefit of his crew.

4.   Loyalty and trust:

Trust and loyalty are essential for the success of a pirate crew. Pirates must be able to rely on each other in order to survive and thrive in the harsh and unpredictable world of piracy. This principle is reflected in the code's emphasis on mutual trust and support among crew members. Famous pirate Henry Morgan is a prime example of this principle in action, as he was known for his strong leadership and his ability to inspire loyalty and trust among his crew.

5.   Discipline and order:

Pirates must be disciplined and follow a set of rules in order to maintain order and ensure the safety of the crew. This principle is reflected in the code's emphasis on strict adherence to rules and guidelines. Famous pirate Bartholomew Roberts, also known as Black Bart, was known for his strict adherence to these rules and for his fair distribution of loot among his crew.

6.   Shared Success and wealth :

The pirates code also emphasizes the importance of shared success and wealth among the crew members. This principle ensures that all members of the crew are rewarded for their hard work and contributions, and that no one individual profits at the expense of others. Famous pirate Francis Drake is a prime example of this principle in action, as he was known for his fair distribution of loot among his crew and his ability to unite them towards a common goal.

7. Equality and democracy:

The pirates code also emphasizes the importance of equality and democracy among the crew members. This principle ensures that all members of the crew have a say in the direction of the ship and that decisions are made through a vote among the crew members. This ensures that all members of the crew feel valued and heard, and that the crew functions as a cohesive unit. Famous pirate Calico Jack is a prime example of this principle in action, as his crew was known for its democratic system of governance and its equality among members.

8.   Honesty and integrity:

The pirates code also emphasizes the importance of honesty and integrity among the crew members. This principle ensures that all members of the crew are truthful and trustworthy, and that they uphold a strong moral code. Famous pirate Henry Every, also known as Henry Avery, is a prime example of this principle in action, as he was known for his honesty and integrity during his time as a pirate. He was able to gain the trust of his crew and his fellow pirates, and his success as a pirate was largely attributed to his strong moral code.

The success of pirates living by the code can be seen throughout history, in the form of famous pirate crews that were known for their strong adherence to the principles of the code. One such example is the crew of William Kidd, also known as Captain Kidd. His crew was known for its strict adherence to the code, and as a result, they were able to achieve great success in their piracy endeavors. They were able to successfully raid multiple ships, and were able to amass a large amount of loot and wealth.

Another example of success can be seen in the crew of Edward Teach, also known as Blackbeard. His crew was known for its strong sense of camaraderie and mutual respect, which was a result of Blackbeard's fair and just leadership. This sense of unity and trust among the crew helped them to achieve great success in their piracy endeavors, and they were able to successfully raid multiple ships and amass a large amount of wealth while gaining a legendary reputation.

In conclusion, the success of pirates living by the code can be seen throughout history, in the form of famous pirate crews that were known for their strong adherence to the principles of the code. These crews were able to achieve great success in their piracy endeavors, due to their strong sense of unity, trust, and discipline. The principles of the code, such as fairness, self-reliance, and honesty, played a crucial role in their success and continue to inspire modern-day leaders and individuals alike.

"Better to live one year as a tiger, than a hundred as a sheep."

- Grace O'Malley, also known as Gráinne Mhaol, a legendary Irish pirate queen

Chapter 3: Taking Control of Your Life

The principles of the pirates code can be applied not just to the life of a pirate, but also to everyday life. By embracing the principles of fairness, self-reliance, and risk-taking, individuals can take control of their own lives and chart their own course to success.

One key principle of the pirates code is self-reliance. This means taking responsibility for your own life and making your own decisions, rather than relying on others to make choices for you. To take control of your life, it is important to set your own goals and work towards achieving them. This could mean going back to school, starting your own business, or pursuing a new hobby. Whatever your goals may be, it is important to have a clear plan and take action towards achieving them. An example of this principle in action is when an individual decides to change career paths. Instead of relying on someone else to make the decision for them, they take the initiative to research different industries, network, and apply for jobs until they find the perfect fit for them.

Another important principle of the pirates code is fairness. This means treating others with respect and ensuring that everyone is treated equally. In order to take control of your life, it is important to surround yourself with people who will support and encourage you, rather than those who will hold you back. This could mean ending toxic relationships or finding a new group of friends who share your goals and values. An example of this principle in action is when an individual realizes that the group of friends they've been hanging out with for years is holding them back from achieving their goals, they make the decision to distance themselves and find a new group of friends who align with their values and support their goals.

Risk-taking is also an essential principle of the pirates code. This means being willing to take risks in order to achieve your goals. In order to take control of your life, it is important to be open to new opportunities and to not be afraid of failure. This could mean taking a chance on a new job opportunity, starting your own business, or pursuing a new hobby. By taking risks, you open yourself up to new experiences and opportunities for growth and success. An example of this principle in action is when an individual decides to leave their stable job to start their own business venture, despite the uncertainty and risk that comes with it. They believe in their idea and are willing to take the risk to make it a success.

In addition to these principles, it is important to also practice discipline and order. This means setting boundaries and sticking to a schedule in order to achieve your goals. This could mean setting aside specific time each day to work on your goals, creating a budget to manage your finances, or developing a workout routine to stay healthy and fit. By being disciplined and organized, you are able to prioritize what is important and make progress towards your goals. An example of this principle in action is when an individual sets a daily schedule for themselves to work on their goals, such as waking up early to work on their business plan or setting aside time in the evening to study for a certification exam.

Furthermore, the principle of shared success and wealth is also important to take control of your life. This means being willing to share your success and to help others achieve their own goals. This can be achieved by mentoring others, collaborating with others on a project, or volunteering your time to help others. By sharing your success and knowledge, you not only help others but also get to learn from others and grow yourself. An example of this principle in action is when a successful entrepreneur takes on an mentee, sharing their knowledge and experience to help them achieve their own success.

Lastly, it's important to have an attitude of honesty and integrity in order to take control of your life. This means being true to yourself and your values, and being accountable for your actions. It also means being honest with yourself about your strengths and weaknesses, and working on the areas that need improvement. This principle is important for building a strong sense of self-awareness and personal responsibility, which are crucial for achieving your goals. An example of this principle in action is when an individual takes a step back to reflect on their actions and realizes that they have been dishonest with themselves about their capabilities and decides to work on themselves to be more honest and improve in that area.

It's important to note that taking control of your life doesn't happen overnight, it's a continuous journey of self-discovery and self-improvement. The principles of the pirates code are a guide, but it's up to each individual to apply them in their own way and at their own pace. It's important to be patient with yourself and to not be too hard on yourself when things don't go as planned. Remember that failure is a part of the process and it's through failure that we learn and grow.

Additionally, it's important to remember that taking control of your life also means being adaptable and flexible. Life is unpredictable and things can change quickly. It's important to be able to adapt to new situations and to be open to new opportunities. The pirates code stresses the importance of being able to navigate through the unknown and to be able to adapt to new surroundings.

In order to take control of your life, it's important to have a clear vision of what you want to achieve, and to have a plan to achieve it. It's also important to surround yourself with people who support and encourage you. It's crucial to build a strong support system of friends and family who will help you through the ups and downs of life. Remember that taking control of your life is not a one-time event, it's a continuous journey. Embrace the principles of the pirates code, be patient with yourself, adaptable to new situations, and always strive to improve yourself and your surroundings.

In conclusion, the principles of the pirates code can be applied to everyday life to help individuals take control of their own lives. By embracing self-reliance, fairness, risk-taking, discipline and order, shared success, and honesty and integrity, individuals can set and achieve their own goals, and live a life of adventure and success. The examples in this chapter are designed to help you understand how these principles can be applied in real-life situations and how they can lead to personal growth and success.

"Without a compass, you're lost at sea. Without a leader, your crew's lost at sea."

- William Kidd, also known as Captain Kidd

Chapter 4: Developing Leadership Skills

The principles of the pirates code, such as fairness, self-reliance, and risk-taking, also apply to leadership. By embracing these principles and developing leadership skills, individuals can become effective leaders and inspire others to achieve their goals.

One key aspect of leadership is the ability to inspire and motivate others. This means being able to clearly communicate your vision and goals, and to rally others to join you in achieving them. To develop this skill, it is important to have a clear understanding of your own values and goals, and to be able to articulate them in a way that resonates with others. It's also important to be able to listen to others and to be open to feedback and new ideas. Famous pirate, Henry Morgan is a prime example of this principle in action, as he was able to inspire his crew and lead them to success through his clear vision and ability to communicate and listen.

Another important leadership skill is the ability to make tough decisions and to take responsibility for the outcome. This means being able to weigh the options and to make the best decision, even when it is not the most popular one. To develop this skill, it is important to be able to think critically and to be able to consider different perspectives. It's also important to be able to accept responsibility for the outcome and to learn from mistakes. Famous pirate, William Kidd, also known as Captain Kidd is a prime example of this principle in action, as he was known for his ability to make tough decisions and take responsibility for the outcome, even when it resulted in failure.

Leadership also involves the ability to build trust and loyalty among your team. This means being able to create an environment where team members feel heard, respected, and valued. To develop this skill, it is important to be able to communicate effectively, to be fair and consistent in your treatment of team members, and to be able to build strong relationships. Famous pirate, Edward Teach, also known as Blackbeard, is a prime example of this principle in action, as he was able to build trust and loyalty among his crew through his fair and just leadership.

In addition to these skills, it's also important for leaders to be able to inspire and lead by example. This means being able to lead by example by setting a positive example of behavior and work ethic. This can be achieved by being disciplined, honest, and diligent in your work. Famous pirate, Anne Bonny is a perfect example of this principle in action, as she was a fierce leader who lead by example and was known for her hard work and dedication.

In conclusion, by embracing the principles of the pirates code, individuals can develop leadership skills and inspire others to achieve their goals. Leadership involves the ability to inspire and motivate others, make tough decisions, build trust and loyalty, and lead by example. These skills can be developed through practice and by embracing the principles of the pirates code, such as fairness, self-reliance, and risk-taking. To become an effective leader, it's important to have a clear understanding of your own values and goals, and to be able to communicate them in a way that resonates with others. It's also important to be able to think critically, make tough decisions, and take responsibility for the outcome. Building trust and loyalty among team members is also crucial for success, and this can be achieved through effective communication, fair and consistent treatment of team members, and strong relationships. Finally, leading by example is crucial for inspiring and motivating others, and this can be achieved by being disciplined, honest, and diligent in your work.

"Victory awaits him who has everything in order, luck, people call it. Defeat is certain for him who has neglected to take the necessary precautions in time; this is called bad luck."

- Roche Braziliano

Chapter 5: Planning for Success

The principles of the pirates code and the leadership skills developed in chapter 4 serve as a guide, but it's important to also have a plan in place in order to achieve success. Planning is a crucial step in the process of taking control of your life and achieving your goals.

The first step in planning for success is to set clear and achievable goals. This means identifying what you want to achieve and setting specific, measurable, and time-bound goals. For example, instead of setting a general goal to "get in shape," a specific goal would be to "lose 10 pounds in 3 months by working out 3 times a week and following a healthy diet." Setting clear and achievable goals will give you something to work towards and will help you stay motivated.

Once you have set your goals, it's important to create a plan of action. This means identifying the steps you need to take in order to achieve your goals. For example, if your goal is to start your own business, your plan of action might include conducting market research, creating a business plan, and networking with potential investors. Having a plan of action will help you stay on track and will make it easier to measure your progress.

Another important aspect of planning for success is to be prepared for obstacles and setbacks. This means having a contingency plan in place in case things don't go as planned. For example, if your goal is to save money, it's important to have a plan in place in case of unexpected expenses or loss of income. Being prepared for obstacles and setbacks will help you to stay resilient and to continue working towards your goals.

In addition to setting goals, creating a plan of action, and being prepared for obstacles and setbacks, it's also important to regularly review and adjust your plan as needed. This means regularly checking in on your progress and making adjustments as needed. For example, if your goal is to lose weight, but you're not seeing the results you want, it's important to review your plan and make adjustments, such as increasing your workout frequency or trying a different diet.

Another important aspect of planning for success is to surround yourself with the right people. This means building a supportive network of friends and colleagues who will help you to achieve your goals. This could include seeking out mentors or joining professional organizations, as well as building supportive relationships with family and friends. Having a strong support system will not only provide you with the encouragement and motivation you need to achieve your goals, but it will also give you access to valuable resources and knowledge. Famous pirate, Francis Drake, is a prime example of this principle in action, as he was able to achieve his goals by surrounding himself with a skilled and loyal crew.

Time management is also a critical component of planning for success. This means using your time effectively in order to achieve your goals. This could include setting a schedule, breaking your goals down into smaller, manageable tasks, and prioritizing the most important tasks. It's important to avoid procrastination and distractions, and to stay focused on your goals. By managing your time effectively, you will be able to make progress towards your goals and achieve success.

Another important aspect of planning for success is to stay positive and have a growth mindset. This means having a positive attitude and being open to new experiences and opportunities. It also means being willing to learn from your mistakes and to see failure as an opportunity to grow and improve. By staying positive and having a growth mindset, you will be able to overcome obstacles and achieve your goals. Famous pirate, Bartholomew Roberts, is a prime example of this principle in action, as he was able to achieve great success despite facing many obstacles, due to his positive attitude and willingness to learn and improve.

Remember to stay true to the principles of the pirates code, such as fairness, self-reliance, and risk-taking, while applying the leadership skills you've learned in chapter 4. With a clear plan and determination, you'll be able to navigate through whatever challenges come your way and chart your own course to success.

In conclusion, planning for success is crucial for achieving your goals. By setting clear and achievable goals, creating a plan of action, being prepared for obstacles and setbacks, regularly reviewing and adjusting your plan, surrounding yourself with the right people, managing your time effectively, and staying positive and having a growth mindset, you'll be able to navigate through the unknown and chart your own course to success. Remember to always stay true to the principles of the pirates code and to apply the leadership skills you've learned in previous chapters. With a clear plan, determination, and the right mindset, you will be able to achieve success in all areas of your life. It's important to remember that planning for success is not a one-time event, but a continuous process. As you achieve your goals, you'll need to set new ones and continue to plan for success. It's important to stay flexible, adapt to changes, and be open to new opportunities. Remember to always stay true to yourself and your values, and to not be afraid to take risks and chart your own course. With a clear plan and the right mindset, you will be able to achieve success and live a life of adventure and fulfillment.

"Keep your face always toward the sunshine - and shadows will fall behind you."

- Blackbeard, or Edward Teach

Chapter 6: Creating a Positive Attitude

A positive attitude is essential for achieving success in all areas of life, especially when following the principles of the pirates code and developing leadership skills. A positive attitude can help you to overcome obstacles, stay motivated, and achieve your goals.

One key aspect of creating a positive attitude is to focus on the present and the future, rather than dwelling on the past. This means letting go of past failures and regrets, and focusing on the present and what you can do to achieve your goals in the future. To develop this skill, it's important to practice mindfulness and to be aware of your thoughts and emotions. It's also important to practice gratitude and to focus on the things you are thankful for in your life.

Another important aspect of creating a positive attitude is to surround yourself with positive people. This means spending time with people who are supportive, encouraging, and who share your values and goals. It's also important to avoid negative people and negative influences, as they can bring you down and discourage you from achieving your goals. To develop this skill, it's important to surround yourself with positive role models and to find a supportive community.

It's also important to practice self-care and self-compassion. This means taking care of your physical, emotional, and mental well-being. To develop this skill, it's important to exercise regularly, eat a healthy diet, get enough sleep, and practice self-compassion. It's important to be kind and understanding towards yourself and to not be too hard on yourself when things don't go as planned.

Another key aspect of creating a positive attitude is to be resilient and to not give up easily. This means being able to bounce back from setbacks and to not let obstacles stop you from achieving your goals. To develop this skill, it's important to practice perseverance and to not be afraid of failure. It's also important to have a growth mindset, and to see failure as an opportunity to learn and grow.

In conclusion, creating a positive attitude is essential for achieving success in all areas of life. By focusing on the present and the future, surrounding yourself with positive people, practicing self-care and self-compassion, being resilient, and having a growth mindset, you can develop a positive attitude and overcome obstacles on your journey to success. Remember to always stay true to the principles of the pirates code and to apply the leadership skills you've learned in previous chapters. With a positive attitude, you will be able to approach challenges with a sense of optimism and determination.

It's also important to remember that creating a positive attitude is a continuous process, and it takes time and effort to maintain. It's important to practice positive habits and to be mindful of your thoughts and emotions. You can also try different techniques such as journaling, visualization, or affirmations to help you maintain a positive attitude.

Additionally, it's important to remember that a positive attitude doesn't mean ignoring or denying negative emotions or problems. It's important to acknowledge and process negative emotions and to work through them in a healthy way. A positive attitude is about finding a balance and finding the good in difficult situations.

In order to maintain a positive attitude, it's important to also practice gratitude. This means being thankful for what you have and focusing on the good things in your life. It's easy to get caught up in what we don't have, but practicing gratitude can help shift your focus to the things that you're grateful for and that can boost your mood and help you maintain a positive attitude.

Remember to always stay true to the principles of the pirates code and to apply the leadership skills you've learned in previous chapters. With a positive attitude, you will be able to approach challenges with a sense of optimism and determination and reach your goals.

"Twenty years from now, you will be more disappointed by the things that you didn't do than by the ones you did do. So throw off the bowlines. Sail away from the safe harbor. Catch the trade winds in your sails. Explore. Dream. Discover."

- Grace O'Malley, also known as Gráinne Mhaol

Chapter 7: Exploring New Opportunities

The principles of the pirates code, such as self-reliance, risk-taking, and adaptability, encourage individuals to explore new opportunities and chart their own course in life. By embracing these principles and exploring new opportunities, individuals can expand their horizons and achieve greater success.

One key aspect of exploring new opportunities is to be open-minded and to be willing to step outside of your comfort zone. This means being willing to try new things and to be open to new experiences. To develop this skill, it's important to be curious and to be willing to learn and grow. Famous pirate, Henry Every, is a prime example of this principle in action, as he was known for his willingness to take risks and explore new opportunities.

Another important aspect of exploring new opportunities is to network and to build relationships. This means making connections and building relationships with others who can help you to achieve your goals. To develop this skill, it's important to be outgoing and to be willing to put yourself out there. It's also important to be a good listener and to be able to build trust and loyalty with others. Famous pirate, William Dampier, is a prime example of this principle in action, as he was able to achieve success by building relationships and networking with others.

It's also important to be adaptable and to be able to navigate through the unknown. This means being able to adjust to new situations and to be able to find opportunities in unexpected places. To develop this skill, it important to stay adaptable even in the face of adversity.

Another important aspect of exploring new opportunities is to stay informed and to stay up to date with current trends and developments in your field. This means staying informed about the latest developments in your industry, and also keeping an eye on emerging trends and opportunities. It's important to keep learning, and to be aware of changes in technology, and other factors that may impact your goals and opportunities. This can include staying informed by reading industry publications, attending conferences and networking events, and staying connected with others in your field. Famous pirate, Francis Drake, is a prime example of this principle in action, as he was known for staying informed and up to date with the latest developments in his field, which helped him to navigate and succeed in new opportunities.

In conclusion, exploring new opportunities is an essential part of living by the principles of the pirates code. By being open-minded, networking, adaptable, persistent, informed and keeping a positive attitude, individuals can expand their horizons and achieve greater success. Remember to always stay true to the principles of the pirates code and to apply the leadership skills you've learned in previous chapters. With a willingness to take risks and explore new opportunities, you will be able to chart your own course meeting the demands of life on the way to achieving your goals.

"Flexibility is the key to stability."

- Anne Bonny

Chapter 8: Developing Flexibility in Leadership

In the world of piracy, leadership requires a unique set of skills and characteristics. One of the most important of these is flexibility. The ability to adapt to changing circumstances and to think on one's feet is essential for successfully leading a crew and navigating the unknown waters of piracy.

One key aspect of developing flexibility in leadership is the ability to make quick and decisive decisions. As a pirate leader, one must be able to make decisions quickly and effectively in order to navigate through dangerous waters and respond to unexpected challenges. This means having the ability to assess a situation, weigh the options, and make a decision, even in the face of uncertainty. Famous pirate, Blackbeard, is a prime example of this principle in action, as he was known for his quick and decisive decision making skills, which helped him to navigate through dangerous waters and outsmart his enemies.

Another important aspect of developing flexibility in leadership is the ability to adapt to different personalities and styles. As a pirate leader, one must be able to lead a diverse crew of individuals with different backgrounds, skills and personalities. This means having the ability to understand and work with different personalities and to use different leadership styles to get the best out of each crew member. Famous pirate, Anne Bonny, is a prime example of this principle in action, as she was able to adapt to different personalities and styles, which helped her to lead a diverse crew and achieve success.

It's also important to be adaptable and to be able to navigate through the unknown. This means being able to adjust to new situations and to be able to find opportunities in unexpected places. To develop this skill, it's important to be resourceful and to be able to think on your feet. It's also important to be able to take advantage of unexpected opportunities and to be able to pivot and make changes when necessary. Famous pirate, Henry Every, is a prime example of this principle in action, as he was able to adapt to new situations and to make the most of unexpected opportunities.

In conclusion, developing flexibility in leadership is an essential part of being a successful pirate leader. By being able to make quick and decisive decisions, adapt to different personalities and styles, and navigate through the unknown, pirate leaders can effectively lead their crew and achieve success. Remember to always stay true to the principles of the pirates code and leverage the leadership skills you've learned in previous chapters. With flexibility, you will be able to navigate through the unknown waters of piracy and chart your own course to success.

"Adversity is a good teacher."
- Sir Francis Drake

Chapter 9: Dealing with Adversity

In the world of piracy, adversity is a constant companion. Whether it be dealing with harsh weather conditions, navigating treacherous waters, or facing off against rival pirate crews, pirate leaders must be able to deal with adversity in order to succeed.

One key aspect of dealing with adversity is to have a strong sense of resilience. This means being able to bounce back from setbacks and to not let obstacles stop you from achieving your goals. To develop this skill, it's important to practice perseverance and to not be afraid of failure. It's also important to have a growth mindset, and to see failure as an opportunity to learn and grow. Famous pirate, Edward Teach, also known as Blackbeard, is a prime example of this principle in action, as he was known for his resilience and determination to achieve his goals, even in the face of adversity.

Another important aspect of dealing with adversity is to have a strong sense of resourcefulness. This means being able to think creatively and to find solutions in unexpected places. To develop this skill, it's important to be able to think on your feet and to be able to adapt to new situations. It's also important to be able to make the most of limited resources and to be able to find opportunities in unexpected places. Famous pirate, William Dampier, is a prime example of this principle in action, as he was able to achieve success by being resourceful and finding opportunities in unexpected places.

It's also important to have a strong sense of teamwork and to be able to work well with others. This means being able to build a strong and loyal crew, and to be able to work together to achieve a common goal. To develop this skill, it's important to be a good listener, to be able to build trust and loyalty, and to be able to work well with others. Famous pirate, Francis Drake, is a prime example of this principle in action, as he was able to achieve success by building a strong and loyal crew and working well with others.

In conclusion, dealing with adversity is an essential part of being a successful pirate leader. By having a strong sense of resilience, resourcefulness, teamwork, and being able to think creatively, pirate leaders can effectively navigate through adversity and achieve success. With the ability to deal with adversity, you will be able to chart your own course through stormy waters and reach your goals, even in the face of challenges.

"A crew is only as strong as its captain and it's unity."

- Bartholomew Roberts.

Chapter 10: Working as a Team

In the world of piracy, the ability to work as a team is essential for achieving success. Whether it be navigating treacherous waters, facing off against rival pirate crews, or dividing up the loot, pirate leaders must be able to work effectively with their crew in order to succeed.

One key aspect of working as a team is to have a clear and shared vision. This means having a common goal and a shared understanding of what the crew is working towards. To develop this skill, it's important to be able to communicate effectively and to be able to inspire and motivate others. Famous pirate, Henry Every, is a prime example of this principle in action, as he was able to achieve success by having a clear and shared vision and inspiring and motivating his crew.

Another important aspect of working as a team is to have a strong sense of trust and loyalty. This means being able to build trust and loyalty among crew members and to be able to rely on one another in difficult situations. To develop this skill, it's important to be trustworthy, to be able to build trust and loyalty, and to be able to rely on others. Famous pirate, Anne Bonny, is a prime example of this principle in action, as she was able to achieve success by building a strong sense of trust and loyalty among her crew.

It's also important to have strong leadership skills and to be able to effectively lead the crew. This means being able to make quick and decisive decisions, to be able to navigate through difficult situations and to be able to inspire and motivate others. To develop this skill, it's important to be a strong leader, to be able to make quick and decisive decisions, and to be able to inspire and motivate others. Famous pirate, Blackbeard, is a prime example of this principle in action, as he was able to achieve success by being a strong leader and effectively leading his crew.

In conclusion, working as a team is an essential part of being a successful pirate leader. By having a clear and shared vision, building trust and loyalty among crew members, and having strong leadership skills, pirate leaders can effectively work with their crew and achieve success. Note to stay true to the principles of the pirates code and to apply the leadership skills you've learned in previous chapters. With the ability to work as a team, you will be able to chart your own course and reach your goals, even in the face of challenges.

"Fortune always favors the brave."

- Anne Bonny

Chapter 11: Overcoming Challenges

In the world of piracy, overcoming challenges is a constant part of the journey. Whether it be dealing with harsh weather conditions, navigating treacherous waters, or facing off against rival pirate crews, pirate leaders must be able to overcome challenges in order to succeed. These same principles can be applied to overcoming challenges in the modern world.

One key aspect of overcoming challenges is to have a strong sense of self-reliance and self-motivation. This means being able to rely on oneself and to be able to push through difficult situations. To develop this skill, it's important to be able to set goals and to be able to motivate oneself to achieve them. Famous pirate, Francis Drake, is a prime example of this principle in action, as he was able to achieve success by being self-reliant and self-motivated, and he set clear goals for himself.

Another important aspect of overcoming challenges is to have a strong sense of adaptability. This means being able to adjust to new situations and to be able to find opportunities in unexpected places. To develop this skill, it's important to be resourceful, and to be able to think on one's feet. Famous pirate, William Dampier, is a prime example of this principle in action, as he was able to achieve success by being adaptable and finding opportunities in unexpected places.

It's also important to have a positive attitude, and to not give up easily. This means being able to bounce back from setbacks and to not let obstacles stop you from achieving your goals. To develop this skill, it's important to be resilient, to have a growth mindset, and to see failure as an opportunity to learn and grow. Famous pirate, Edward Teach, also known as Blackbeard, is a prime example of this principle in action, as he was known for his persistence and determination to achieve his goals, even in the face of adversity.

In the modern world, these principles can be applied to overcoming challenges such as career setbacks, personal obstacles, or navigating a rapidly changing business environment. By being self-reliant, adaptable, and having a positive attitude, individuals can push through difficult situations and find success in the face of challenges.

In conclusion, overcoming challenges is an essential part of being a successful pirate leader, and also in achieving success in the modern world. By being self-reliant, adaptable, and having a positive attitude, individuals can push through difficult situations and find success. Remember with the ability to overcome challenges, you will be able to chart your own course and reach your goals, even in the face of adversity.

"Life is either a daring adventure or nothing at all."

- Edward Teach, also known as Blackbeard

Chapter 12: Applying the Pirates Code to Your Life

The Pirates Code is not just a set of rules for pirates, it is a way of life that can be applied to modern day living for achieving success and living life to the fullest. The principles of the code, such as taking control of your own destiny, being adaptable, and having a positive attitude, are universal and timeless, and can be applied to any individual looking to live an adventurous and fulfilling life.

One key aspect of applying the Pirates Code to your life is to view it as an adventure. This means embracing new experiences, taking risks and not being afraid to step out of your comfort zone. Famous pirate, Anne Bonny, is a prime example of this principle in action, as she took control of her own destiny and lived an adventurous life as a pirate, breaking societal norms and expectations.

Another important aspect of applying the Pirates Code to your life is to be open to new opportunities. This means being able to adjust to new situations and to be able to find opportunities in unexpected places. Famous pirate, Henry Every, is a prime example of this principle in action, as he was able to achieve success by being adaptable and finding opportunities in unexpected places, such as capturing a Mughal ship, which was one of the most profitable pirate raids in history.

It's also important to have a positive attitude and to not give up easily. This means being able to bounce back from setbacks and to not let obstacles stop you from achieving your goals. To develop this skill, it's important to be resilient, to have a growth mindset, and to see failure as an opportunity to learn and grow. Famous pirate,

Bartholomew Roberts, is a prime example of this principle in action, as he was known for his persistence and determination to achieve his goals, even in the face of adversity.

Applying the Pirates Code to your life can be a powerful tool for achieving success and living life to the fullest. By viewing life as an adventure, being open to new opportunities, and having a positive attitude, individuals can chart their own course and reach their goals, even in the face of adversity. Remember to always stay true to the principles of the pirates code and to apply the leadership skills you've learned in previous chapters. With the right mindset, the possibilities are endless.

Another key principle of the Pirates Code is to work as a team. This means valuing the contributions of others and working together towards a common goal. Famous pirate, Blackbeard, is a prime example of this principle in action, as he was known for his ability to lead and inspire his crew, and for fostering a sense of camaraderie among his men.

Leadership skills are also crucial in applying the Pirates Code to your life. This means being able to inspire and guide others, as well as being able to make difficult decisions. Famous pirate, Edward Teach, also known as Blackbeard, is a prime example of this principle in action, as he was a charismatic leader who was able to inspire loyalty and respect among his crew.

By embracing the principles of the Pirates Code, you can take control of your life, develop leadership skills, and achieve success. Whether you're an entrepreneur, a student, or a professional, the same principles can be applied to your life to help you achieve your goals and live life to the fullest.

"The world is full of opportunities, my friend. It's up to you whether or not you seize them."

- Anne Bonny

Final words

In conclusion, applying the Pirates Code to your life is about taking control of your destiny, being adaptable, having a positive attitude, working as a team, developing leadership skills and planning for success. By embracing the principles of the Pirates Code, you can not only achieve success but also live a more fulfilling life. Remember, life is an adventure, and the Pirates Code is the map that can guide you to the treasure of your dreams.

The Pirates Code is not just a set of rules for pirates, it is a way of life that can be applied to modern day living for achieving success and living life to the fullest. The principles of the code, such as taking control of your own destiny, being adaptable, having a positive attitude, working as a team, developing leadership skills, and planning for success, are universal and timeless. By embracing these principles, individuals can chart their own course and reach their goals, even in the face of adversity.

The key to applying the Pirates Code to your life is to view it as an adventure. This means embracing new experiences, taking risks, and not being afraid to step out of your comfort zone. Famous pirates like Anne Bonny, Henry Every, Bartholomew Roberts and Blackbeard are prime examples of this principle in action, as they took control of their own destinies and lived adventurous lives, breaking societal norms and expectations.

The Pirates Code is a reminder that life is meant to be lived as an adventure and not to be wasted on the sidelines. Like the pirates who sailed the seas in search of their treasure, you too can chart your own course and find the treasure of your dreams. Embrace the principles of the Pirates Code and you will find that the possibilities are endless.

The Pirates Code is a powerful guide to taking control of your life, developing leadership skills, planning for success, and embracing a positive attitude, even in the face of adversity. By embracing these principles, you too can live a life of purpose, fulfillment, and success.

Whether you are an entrepreneur, student, or professional, the Pirates Code provides valuable lessons that can be applied to your life to help you achieve your goals and live life to the fullest. Remember, life is an adventure and, much like the pirates of old, you have the power to chart your own course and seek out the treasures of your dreams.

So, embrace the Pirates Code and make your life an adventure. Be daring, be bold, and take control of your destiny. Live life to the fullest and discover the riches that await you along the way. Arrr!

A example of codes to live by:

1. "I am the captain of my own ship, charting my own course in life and facing every challenge with boldness and determination."

2. "I live by the code of the pirate, embracing freedom, adventure, and the pursuit of success in all aspects of my life."

3. "I take control of my life and chart my own path, never shying away from risks and always seeking new opportunities."

4. "I lead by example, inspiring others to join me on my quest for greatness and embracing the principles of the Pirates Code in all I do."

5. "I am resilient, adapting to the winds of change and facing adversity with the same courage and determination as the greatest pirates of old."

6. "I work as a team, relying on the support of those around me and always striving to build strong and lasting relationships."

7. "I overcome challenges, pushing past my limits and emerging stronger and more determined to succeed."

8. "I embrace the spirit of adventure, living life to the fullest and never giving up in the pursuit of my dreams."

9. "I am a pirate, always pushing boundaries and exploring new frontiers in life and in leadership."

10. "I live by the Pirates Code, embracing the principles of freedom, resilience, leadership, and success in all I do."

A set of guiding principles for those chose the to live by the code:

1. Embrace freedom: Live life on your own terms, unencumbered by the opinions and expectations of others.

2. Pursue adventure: Embrace the unknown, seek out new challenges, and never stop exploring.

3. Take control: Take charge of your own life, make your own decisions, and chart your own course.

4. Lead by example: Inspire others with your actions, and set an example for the world to follow.

5. Be resilient: Adapt to changing circumstances, face adversity with courage, and never give up.

6. Work as a team: Build strong relationships, support those around you, and always strive to bring out the best in others.

7. Overcome challenges: Face difficulties head-on, push past your limits, and emerge stronger and more determined.

8. Cultivate a positive attitude: See the world through a lens of hope and possibility, and always strive to find the best in every situation.

9. Embrace new opportunities: Take chances, try new things, and never be afraid to fail.

10. Live life to the fullest: Enjoy every moment, embrace the adventure of life, and never stop seeking new experiences.

Set of Questions to ask yourself when setting your own Pirate Code to live by:

1. What are your core values and principles?

2. What are the things you stand for, and what motivates you to take action?

3. What are your strengths and weaknesses as a person?

4. How can you use your strengths to your advantage, and what can you do to overcome your weaknesses?

5. How do you want to be perceived by others, and what kind of legacy do you want to leave behind?

6. What kind of impact do you want to make on the world around you?

7. What are your long-term goals, and what steps can you take to achieve them?

8. What kind of progress do you want to make in your personal and professional life, and how can you stay motivated and focused?

9. How do you want to treat others, and what kind of relationships do you want to have with the people in your life?

10. How can you cultivate a sense of community and connection with those around you?

11. What do you want to do with your life, and what kind of adventures and experiences do you want to have?

12. How can you embrace new opportunities and live life to the fullest?

13. What are the things you won't compromise on, and what are the lines you won't cross?

14. What are the things that are non-negotiable for you, and how can you stay true to your values and beliefs?

15. How do you want to respond to adversity and challenges, and what kind of mindset do you want to cultivate?

16. How can you stay resilient and adaptable in the face of setbacks and obstacles?

17. What kind of code of conduct do you want to live by, and how can you hold yourself accountable to it?

18. How can you stay true to your word and honor your commitments?

19. How can you balance your personal desires and ambitions with your obligations to others and the world around you?

20. How can you find a sense of harmony and balance in your life?

"Life is too short to waste. Time is too precious to be spent on anything other than living to the fullest."

- Jack Sparrow

Quotes to live your days by:

Days of the Month:

1. "**Life's pretty good, and why wouldn't it be? I'm a pirate, after all.**"
    - Johnny Depp as Jack Sparrow

2. "**Life is either a daring adventure or nothing.**" *- Anne Bonny*

3. "**To live life without adventure is to live a life without meaning.**"
    - Blackbeard

4. "**Life is a journey, not a destination.**"
    - William Kidd, also known as Captain Kidd

5. **"The purpose of life is to live it, to taste experience to the utmost, to reach out eagerly and without fear for newer and richer experience."**
    - Henry Morgan

6. **"Life is short, and the world is wide."**
    - Simon Duff

7. **"The sea is a dangerous place, but it's also a place of great adventure and opportunity."** *- Grace O'Malley*

8. **"Life is too short to waste time on things that don't matter."**
    - Calico Jack Rackham

9. **"Life is not a problem to be solved, but a reality to be experienced."**
   - *Edward Teach, also known as Blackbeard*

10. **"Every man has a price he will willingly accept, even for the loss of his soul. Life itself is not priceless."**
    - *Bartholomew Roberts*

11. **"Life is like a sea voyage, full of storms and dangers, but also full of beauty and adventure."**
    - *François l'Olonnais*

12. **"The greatest glory in living lies not in never falling, but in rising every time we fall."** - *Ching Shih*

13. **"Life is a journey, and every journey has a story."** - *Mary Read*

14. **"Life is too important to be taken seriously."** - *Captain Hook*

15. **"The best things in life are the people we love, the places we've been, and the memories we've made along the way."** - *Captain Flint*

16. **"The most valuable thing in life is freedom, the freedom to choose your own path and live your life on your own terms."** - *Anne Bonny*

17. **"Life is an adventure, so don't be afraid to take risks and follow your dreams."** - *William Kidd, also known as Captain Kidd*

18. **"Life is about creating and living experiences that are worth sharing."**
- Blackbeard

19. **"Life is full of surprises, so be prepared to adapt and embrace the unexpected."** *- Grace O'Malley.*

20. **"Life is what you make it, so make it one worth remembering."**
- *Calico Jack Rackham*

21. **"Life is a journey, not a destination, so make the most of every moment."**
- *Calico Jack Rackham*

22. **"Life is short, so live it to the fullest and don't take anything for granted."** *- Bartholomew Roberts*

23. **"Life is about taking chances and living without regrets."** - *Mary Read*

24. **"Life is precious, so make every day count and leave your mark on the world." -** *Edward Teach, also known as Blackbeard*

25. **"Life is an adventure, so don't be afraid to set sail and explore the unknown."** - *Francois l'Olonnais*

26. **"Life is not about waiting for the storm to pass, it's about learning to dance in the rain."** - *Pirate proverb*

27. **"Life is a journey that's meant to be shared with others, so make the most of your relationships."** - *Anne Bonny*

28. **"Life is about facing your fears and having the courage to overcome them."**
- William Kidd, also known as Captain Kidd

29. **"Life is an opportunity, seize it with both hands and don't let go."**
- Black Bart Roberts

30. **"Life is about pursuing your passions and living your dreams, no matter how difficult the journey may be."**
- Grace O'Malley

31. **"Life is what you make of it, so don't waste a moment and create the life you desire."** *- Benjamin Hornigold*

Bonus Chapter: The Pirates Code and Setting Goals

In this bonus chapter, we'll explore how the Pirates Code can help us set and achieve our goals. Like pirates, we all have dreams and aspirations that we want to achieve, but sometimes we may feel overwhelmed and unsure of how to get there. By following the principles of the Pirates Code, we can chart our course and navigate the uncertain waters of life to reach our desired destination.

Visualize Your Success

Before setting any goals, it's essential to have a clear vision of what success looks like to you. Just like a pirate captain setting sail for treasure, you need to have a clear picture of what you want to achieve. Take some time to visualize your desired outcome in as much detail as possible. What does it look, feel, and sound like? What steps did you take to get there? Who helped you along the way? By creating a vivid mental image of your success, you'll have a better understanding of the steps you need to take to make it a reality.

Set Specific and Measurable Goals

Pirates were experts at setting specific and measurable goals. They knew exactly how much treasure they wanted to plunder and how they would divide it among the crew. Similarly, we need to set clear and specific goals that are measurable and achievable. Rather than setting a vague goal like "I want to be successful," break it down into smaller, specific steps that you can track and measure. For example, "I want to increase my sales by 20% over the next six months by acquiring three new clients per month."

Stay Focused and Motivated

As with any long journey, there will be challenges and setbacks along the way. Pirates faced rough seas, storms, and enemy ships, but they persevered by staying focused and motivated on their ultimate goal. Similarly, we need to stay motivated and focused on our goals, even when the going gets tough. Celebrate small victories along the way and use them as motivation to keep pushing forward.

Take Action and Adjust Course

Pirates were not afraid to take action and make adjustments along the way. They knew that they needed to adapt to changing circumstances to reach their goal. Similarly, we need to take action towards our goals and adjust course as necessary. If a particular strategy isn't working, try something new. Don't be afraid to take risks and make changes to your plan as needed.

Work as a Team

Pirates were a tight-knit community that worked together towards a common goal. They knew that they couldn't achieve their goals alone and relied on their crew for support and assistance. Similarly, we need to work as a team towards our goals. Surround yourself with supportive people who will encourage and motivate you along the way. Don't be afraid to ask for help when you need it.

By following the Pirates Code and these principles for goal setting, we can chart a course towards success and navigate the uncertain waters of life. Like pirates, we can set our sights on the horizon, take action towards our goals, and celebrate our victories along the way. With determination, focus, and teamwork, we can achieve our dreams and live a life full of adventure and success.

In conclusion, building goals and living by a code in life can be instrumental in achieving success. By setting specific, measurable, achievable, relevant, and time-bound goals, you can ensure that you are on track towards achieving what you desire. Additionally, by creating a code of conduct for yourself, you can stay grounded and focused on your values and principles, even in the face of challenges and obstacles.

Success is not just about achieving external rewards or accomplishments; it is also about becoming the best version of yourself and living a life that aligns with your values and purpose. So, as you embark on your journey towards success, remember to keep your goals and code in mind, and to stay committed to the process, no matter what comes your way.

Ultimately, success is a journey, not a destination, and it requires dedication, perseverance, and resilience. So, stay focused, stay true to yourself, and never give up on your dreams. With the right mindset and approach, you can achieve anything you set your mind to.

www.ingramcontent.com/pod-product-compliance
Lightning Source LLC
Chambersburg PA
CBHW070406220526
45467CB00001B/487